THE **UN**OFFICIAL GUIDE TO ACHIEVING YOUR GOALS

THE **UN**OFFICIAL GUIDE TO

ACHIEVING YOUR GOALS

Seven Steps
to Creating Your Road Map to
SUCCESS

ONYX JONES

The UNOfficial Guide to Achieving Your Goals
Seven Steps to Creating Your Road Map to Success

iUniverse books may be ordered through booksellers or by contacting:

iUniverse
1663 Liberty Drive
Bloomington, IN 47403
www.iuniverse.com
1-800-Authors (1-800-288-4677)

Because of the dynamic nature of the Internet, any web addresses or links contained in this book may have changed since publication and may no longer be valid. The views expressed in this work are solely those of the author and do not necessarily reflect the views of the publisher, and the publisher hereby disclaims any responsibility for them.

Any people depicted in stock imagery provided by Thinkstock are models, and such images are being used for illustrative purposes only. Certain stock imagery © Thinkstock.

ISBN: 978-1-4917-0806-4 (sc)
ISBN: 978-1-4917-0807-1 (e)

Library of Congress Control Number: 2013917052

Print information available on the last page.

iUniverse rev. date: 10/22/2013

Contents

Introduction ix

Step One   Improve Your Relationships 1
Step Two   Improve Your Spiritual Relationship 9
Step Three   Redefine Your Life's Goals 19
Step Four   Improve Your Talents and Skills.............. 27
Step Five   Make Your Dreams a Reality 33
Step Six   Set Financial Goals 45
Step Seven   Live with Passion 59

About the Author 69

Introduction

This guide is an unconventional, nonphilosophical, and humorous road map to achieving your goals. It is intended to motivate, inspire, and provide you with tools for achieving your goals and living a life of passion. When you read this guide, you must have faith that you have what it takes to experience great success, and you must take action.

Regardless of your economic status or your educational background, this guide will help anyone who has a genuine desire to create a plan for success and is willing to stick to that plan until the goals have been achieved. If you commit to completing the seven steps in this guide, you will have a clear and concise road map to achieving your goals and all the blessings that come with them.

> A goal without a plan is just a wish.
> —Antoine de Saint-Exupery
> *Flight to Arras*, 1942,
> translated from French by Lewis Galantière

If your desire is to live a life filled with passion and prosperity, then this guide will show you how to achieve your goals, whether they are related to your finances, career, business, or education. The seven steps outlined in this guide can change your life by helping you:

1. Select the right goals partner
2. Improve your spiritual life
3. Create new goals or redefine your current goals
4. Improve your talents and skills
5. Identify and focus on steps needed to make your dreams a reality
6. Improve your financial situation
7. Live life with passion

 This seven-step guide outlines a simple and easy way for you to achieve your goals in a positive manner. It really doesn't matter what type of goals you have; the steps in this guide are workable for anyone who wants to create a successful road map. If you follow all seven steps, you will increase the amount of success you will achieve. If you cannot work all seven steps right away, that's okay too. Each step is a building block for the next step. You can work at your own pace and still work toward your goals effectively. I challenge you to make a mental note of where you are in life right now; after reading all seven steps of this guide and committing to following all seven steps, you will see improvement in your quality of life in just thirty to ninety days. You can take all the time you need to complete the steps. The objective is to fulfill your goals in a wildly successful manner in the way that works best for you.

Keep in mind that your success will be long-term if it is achieved with a "good" purpose. So make sure you focus on goals that are positive and have the potential of being a blessing to you, your family, your community, and people that you may never have a chance to meet.

> You are to become a creator, not a competitor;
> you are going to get what you want, but in
> such a way that when you get it every other
> man will have more than he has now.
> —Wallace D. Wattles
> *The Science of Getting Rich*

Now let's start.

Step One

Step one is the most fun; however, for some people, it can also be the most frightening step. If you do step one right, it may lead to wonderful, loving, and supportive relationships. Your first task is to identify someone you already have a good relationship with and invite him or her to be your goals partner and to go through this process with you. Your goals partner could be your husband, wife, fiancé, boyfriend, girlfriend, wannabe boyfriend, or wannabe girlfriend. The key here is that you must feel a tremendous amount of energy when you are around your goals partner, and he or she must support you, believe in you, and inspire you.

A goals partner can also be any person whom you have a close relationship with (family member, mother, father, sister, brother, grandparent, cousin, close friend, mentor, pastor, ministry leader, or even someone from a support group). The requirement is that he or she is supportive of your dreams and truly inspires you to be great. Your goals partner must be willing to talk to you frequently and to share thoughts and ideas while completing exercises or doing fun activities together. You will also be accountable to your goals partner, so be sure you pick someone who will encourage you to follow through with the road map you choose for yourself.

If you are having difficulty thinking of someone to be your goals partner because you live an independent life, now is the time to step out of your box and learn to trust at least one person in your life. The seven steps outlined in this book will be most effective if you work with a goals partner. You will probably find that the work you do with your goals partner will also help you build stronger relationships.

If you are fiercely independent and are convinced that a goals partner is not for you or you want your partner to be God or your spiritual figure, then go through the seven steps with the use of a journal. If this guide calls for exercises that require work with your goals partner, take time to journal your thoughts and use prayer or meditation to think through the exercises with an open and clear mind. Just make sure you are open to new ideas and willing to do things differently than you have in the past.

Getting Started: Step One
There may be several questions on your mind at this point, like, for example: Why is finding a goals partner so important? What does someone else have to do with me achieving my goals? Don't I have to do all the work? Why do I need other people?

A great amount of energy is created when you are working with someone whom you respect and who respects you and you're discussing goals and dreams you have always longed to achieve. A great positive force emanates when two people are sharing love, support, kindness, their experience and knowledge, and encouragement. Many people who have experienced an extreme amount of success in their life tend to give homage to loved ones, friends, and mentors who have supported them along the way.

> Coming together is a beginning.
> Keeping together is progress.
> Working together is success.
> —Henry Ford

> Alone we can do so little; together we can do so much.
> —Helen Keller

Life is just easier when you have someone who genuinely loves and supports you. You can seize new opportunities together. Finding the right person will literally change your life. So how do you know if you have the right goals partner? Here are some tips to consider:

- Do you and your partner have mutual respect for each other? Your partner should be encouraging and honest with you. Your partner must be willing to give constructive criticism when needed and offer praise when deserved.

- Do you and your goals partner communicate well? There are only seven steps in this guide; however, the exercises require that you communicate with your goals partner frequently.

- Does your goals partner have time available to you? As you start generating new ideas and you get excited about sharing insights, you will want to share your thoughts with your goals partner. You don't want to consume all of your goals partner's time, but you will need to share quality time on a schedule that works for both of you.

- Is your goals partner willing to agree to disagree when you don't see eye to eye? You will not always agree on everything as you work through these exercises, so it is important that you respect each other's opinions and can continue to move forward in pursuing your goals with the same amount of support and encouragement.

- Do you and your goals partner share some of the same core values? It's okay if you and your goals partner have different interests and are pursuing different goals; however, there will be unnecessary friction if you have very different core values about life, family, and religion.

- Most importantly, does your goals partner like to have fun? You want to connect with someone who makes you smile and is enjoyable to be around. You will be doing several exercises together, and it should be an enjoyable and fun experience.

Once you have identified the right person to be your goals partner, share this book with him or her. Tell him or her that there are some things you have always wanted to accomplish in life and you have found the tool that will allow you to create a road map to those accomplishments. Ask this person if he or she would be willing to work with you as your goals partner to assist you in achieving your goals. Encourage this person to read this book as well so that he or she can get familiar with the role of the goals partner in your journey to success. It would be even more exciting if your selected person chose to create goals for him- or herself as well. Assure your goals partner that he or she doesn't need to have any special qualifications but just an interest in helping you be successful.

A friend accepts us as we are yet helps
us to be what we should.
—Author Unknown

Assignment One
The assignment for step one is to find someone who makes a good goals partner and request that he or she be your goals partner as you go through the next seven steps of this guide. Remember to find someone who has mutual respect for you, communicates well with you, is available to you, shares some of the same core values as you do, and knows how to have fun.

The next part of assignment one is to find a book on creating and building lasting relationships. *The UNOfficial Guide to Achieving Lasting Relationships* by Onyx Jones is a good example, but any book that discusses how to build and keep lasting relationships will work. Gaining new insight and information is key.

It's not important that you believe everything you read in the book you chose. In fact, you would not be protecting yourself if you believed everything you read. The important thing is that you expand and challenge your mind with new information. As you begin reading your relationship book, journal your responses to items 1-3 listed below. Then schedule some time with your goals partner and discuss your insights or revelations you have discovered in your readings.

1. Find at least five interesting, motivational, or educational things in your reading that you would like to share with your goals partner.

    _____

    _____

    _____

    _____

2. Identify at least one thing that you would like to do or change in your relationships with others to improve your life.

    _____

    _____

    _____

3. Discuss five things that you are thankful for in your relationship with your goals partner or someone special in your life.

    _____

    _____

    _____

The first assignment is to find a goals partner and a book on relationships and read at least fifteen minutes a day. Take time each day to connect with your goals partner and discuss five things, concepts, or ideas that you learned from your book that day. It doesn't matter if you agree with the concept or not. What matters instead is that you and your goals partner share ideas and thoughts in a supportive manner. No one has to be right or wrong. If you picked a good book, the concepts and ideas presented will help you improve your relationship with your goals partner.

As the communication with your goals partner improves and you learn ways of improving your relationship, you will also discover that the things you learn can also help you to be successful in other relationships. If you are married or engaged or dating, your significant other will thank you when he or she sees the positive changes in your life.

Now, for those of you who have decided to do the steps independently, journal your thoughts and meditate, respond to items 1–3, and review your answers a few days later. Take time to challenge yourself. Look at what you wrote and see what you can learn about yourself. Ask yourself why those five things were important to you, and make a commitment to make changes within yourself to improve your relationships.

Achieving your goals will eventually require the help of others along the way; creating positive relationships will only help you in the long run. Creating successful healthy relationships is a vital key to achieving your goals.

Step Two

The first part of step two is to remember step one.
- Read books on relationships (at least fifteen minutes a day).
- Continue to build a great thriving relationship with your goals partner.

It is not okay to give up or delay step one until later. Each step is a building block toward the next, and particularly this first step is key to achieving your goals.

The second part of step two is to create conversations with your higher power. You can try prayer, yoga, meditation, reading, visualization, or the like. Any process that allows your mind time to renew and connect to your higher power will work. This is the time to develop and improve your spiritual life. It doesn't matter what your spiritual life looks like at the moment, just get one if you don't yet have one.

> We are not human beings having a spiritual experience.
> We are spiritual beings having a human experience.
> —Teilhard de Chardin,
> French philosopher

Step two requires that you get to a place where you have constant communication with your higher power. Your conversations with your higher power do not have to be for a specific set time; instead, your goal should be to create a lifestyle where you hear the voice of your higher power throughout the day—while at work, driving in your car, eating dinner, or in the evening instead of watching television. There is no right or wrong way to communicate with your higher power. Some people like to talk out loud, some people prefer to be silent and sit in prayer quietly, and some people seek divine guidance through reading.

Step two is intended solely for you to get in touch with your higher power in any way that is effective for you so that you are clear on your life's purpose and the goals you should strive for while you are here on earth. Step two will expand the traditional view of praying and asking for all your desires and needs. Step two will also help you cut off some of the negative, self-defeating chatter that may go on through your mind and replace it with positive thoughts geared toward achieving your goals.

Getting Started: Step Two
Creating a spiritual relationship with your higher power gets you closer to discovering your true purpose in life. What is the point of achieving your goals when they are not connected to your life's purpose? Achieving goals for the mere sake of gaining material things will leave you unsatisfied and unfulfilled. You must form a clear and definite mental picture of the goals you want to achieve and their significance to your purpose.

You have been placed on this earth to fulfill a purpose. Whether you consider your purpose great or small is in the power of your perception. You possess innate talents that are special and unique to you. If you are able to tap into your talents, you will experience a successful and fulfilling life and career.

It would be profoundly sad if you never discovered what your true natural talents are or if you spent years focusing on enhancing skills that are not connected to your purpose.

> God wants that you should make the most of yourself,
> for yourself, and for others; and you can help others more
> by making the most of yourself than in any other way.
> —Wallace D. Wattles
> *The Science of Getting Rich*

Assignment Two
The assignment for step two is to use your relationship with your higher power to help you identify goals that are connected to your true natural talents and your life's purpose. Take some quiet time, preferably after reading your book on relationships, sit quietly and pray, meditate, or just talk to your higher power.

Your objective will be to write down at least three short-term goals to achieve within the next thirty to ninety days and two long-term goals to achieve within the next six months to a year. The key is that you must be passionate about the goals you set. These goals can be things or activities you never thought you had the time to complete or even start. They should be fun things or activities that are not difficult for you. They can be goals that you have already accomplished with some level of success but you want to take it a level further. The secret here is to spend time in prayer or meditation talking with your higher power and identifying goals that are relevant to your life's purpose.

> You are never too old to set another
> goal or to dream a new dream.
> —C. S. Lewis

Short-Term Goals (Thirty to Ninety Days)

_____

_____

_____

_____

_____

Long-Term Goals (Six Months to a Year)

_____

_____

_____

_____

_____

All super-achievers, please stand down; there are no perks for setting an exorbitant number of goals at one time. You don't get bragging rights if your list is longer than somebody else's.

If you can only come up with goals that seem heavy, uninspiring, and tiresome even when just thinking about them, you may also need to find a book on building spiritual relationships with your higher power. I don't believe anyone's higher power would propose that you set goals that cause depression, frustration, or stress.

Once you have spent time with your higher power in prayer, meditation, or conversation and you have a clear purpose, you may find that you have to set your goals in segments or steps. Say your ultimate purpose or goal in life is to start a construction business that solves a problem for many people. Start with incremental steps that will lead you to your ultimate goal. Here's an example:

ULTIMATE GOAL:	Start a New Construction Business
Step #1	Write an executive summary or a detailed description of what your construction business would look like, which people you would serve, and how the marketing would be done (check out examples of executive summaries on the Internet).
Step #2	Start a savings program to save funds toward the start-up cost (start an automatic transfer of a certain dollar amount into a separate investment account).

Step #3	Research other ways to generate start-up capital for your construction business.
	• Use the Internet.
	• Go to the local bank.
	• Visit the Small Business Association (SBA).
Step #4	Write a dynamic business or marketing plan for your construction business. The plan must provide a detailed description of your business, a description of the services offered, a market analysis, a marketing strategy, a summary of the management, and a financial plan for the first three to five years of operation along with a break-even analysis. This business plan will allow you to go to banks, investors, or even family and friends to request a start-up loan.

The steps you create do not have to be perfect; you just need to write down ways in which you are able to see significant progress in reaching your goals within 90 to 180 days later. The steps you create are significant because they, too, are goals in themselves.

> It is not enough to take steps which may someday lead to a goal; each step must be itself a goal and a step likewise.
> —Johann Wolfgang von Goethe,
> writer, artist, politician

It is also extremely important to write things down rather than just keeping your goals in your head. One of my readers, Stanley, had goals he had wanted to achieve for over ten years, but he was frustrated because he didn't see how he could keep working his business and pursue his goals at the same time. Unfortunately, he only read through step two of this guide, but he did write down a list of five short-term goals. He got too busy with life to continue the step-by-step guide. A year later he came across this guide and started reading where he had left off earlier. When he reread the step two assignment where he had noted five short-term goals the year before, he was amazed to find that he had actually achieved two of his goals. He realized that just by writing the goals down, his goals had become realistic to him. They were no longer a mere fantasy. After that discovery, he finished reading the guide and completed the rest of the steps and assignments. He found that the assignments in the guide allowed him to stay focused on the steps he created toward his goals, and it helped him to achieve even bigger goals at a much faster pace.

So once you've written your steps down and you are very clear on your goals, you must not lose sight of your goals. Do not stop reading and working on the seven steps outlined in this guide. Share your goals with your goals partner and allow him or her to provide feedback. Your goals partner may think about steps that you missed. Your goals partner may provide additional insight on certain talents you have that will make your goals achievable. Your goals partner may even help you redesign your goals so that you can achieve them more quickly. Whatever the case, listen to and accept your goals partner's feedback and see what you can learn from his or her input.

Also, take time to schedule some time where you and your goals partner can go someplace fun and relaxing to discuss the following:

- How will your life be different after your goals are achieved and you are experiencing success?

- Identify any accomplishments you've made so far in completing some or all of the steps toward your goals and celebrate.

- Take time to share your big dreams and to think outside the box.

- Describe to your goals partner what you may look like a year from now when you've successfully achieved each goal.

If you still have not found a goals partner, take out your journal and write down your responses to the discussion items listed above. Be sure you take the time to revisit your journal a few days later; you will be impressed with what you have written. You might even go out on a limb and share what you wrote with someone you trust. It's never too late to find a goals partner as you work through this guide.

At the end of step two, I leave you with two final thoughts. One, you must desire to achieve your goals so badly that you are willing to overcome any obstacles, such as mental or physical complacency. You must be driven to work to obtain your goals no matter what.

Patience, persistence, and perspiration make
an unbeatable combination for success.
—Napoleon Hill

Two, always remember to give thanks to your higher power
with each step you take toward your goals. Gratitude always
generates positive energy, which opens doors and invites
opportunities.

The more gratefully we fix our minds on
the Supreme when good things come to us,
the more good things we will receive.
—Wallace D. Wattles
The Science of Getting Rich

Step Three

The first part of step three is to remember step one and step two.

- Read books on relationships (at least fifteen minutes a day).
- Continue to build a thriving relationship with your goals partner.
- Spend time in prayer or meditation with your higher power.
- Read books that will help you improve your spiritual relationship to your higher power (at least fifteen minutes a day).
- Read and reread your short-term and long-term goals with excitement.

Before you proceed to step three, make sure that you are comfortable with the goals you have created so far. If you're not comfortable or if you haven't come up with any goals at all, let's take a

moment to pause. I was in this situation once: I was so used to helping others achieve their dreams, I couldn't figure out what *I* wanted to do in life. I had a lot of success in my accounting career, but something inside me always knew I was created for other purposes as well.

If you're not sure of your goals, try asking yourself questions like:

- What would I love doing for the next twenty years?
- What things would I like to do even if I never got paid to do them?
- If I were nominated for the Nobel Prize, what would I want to receive it for?
- What have I been putting off for the last year or more?
- What things or activities make me happy?

You may also try watching motivational television shows or reading motivational books and wait for a divine voice to direct you. You can start with one goal and then build from there.

There are numerous ways to connect with your true passion(s) in life, but if you are still drawing a blank and cannot think of any goals that inspire you, proceed to step seven of this guide. However, please make this your last resort, because there is a reason that step seven is at the end of the book.

Once you have at least one goal identified, it's time to proceed with step three. We are going to use step three for visualization exercises to help you see yourself operating in your goals and creating the life that you want. You may not realize it, but you use visualization every day, all the time. There are various forms of visualizations: you may see mental pictures when things are described to you, you may daydream, or you may picture objects or people when they are not in sight. This guide will encourage you to become an expert at creating clear mental pictures of your purpose. Eventually, you will spend more time mentally focusing on achieving your goals.

> First comes thought; then organization of that
> thought, into ideas and plans; then transformation
> of those plans into reality. The beginning, as
> you will observe, is in your imagination.
> —Napoleon Hill

Getting Started: Step Three
There is one thing that has been found to be true in life—in order for something to be physically created on earth, someone had to create it in his or her mind first. Physical inventions are typically visualized by the inventor long before they manifest into something tangible. Blueprints for a building are only created after the architect saw the picture of the building in his or her mind first. Theater performances, movies, and television shows are all created by playwrights and screenwriters who visualized the programs in their minds first. Powerful movements and large organizations were created because people were willing to see things being done differently in the world and they were able to make other people see their vision too.

Visualization is a powerful method of attracting things that you desire to come into your life. When you visualize, you use your imagination to create clear images, ideas, and feelings toward your goals. You should continually put out positive energy toward that goal until it becomes a reality for you.

Let's quickly address those dreaded thoughts of doubt, worry, or concern. Don't try to prevent those thoughts; they are natural. Those and other negative thoughts are probably the reason you have not pursued some of your goals earlier. The best strategy in dealing with those negative thoughts is to identify them and realize that they are thoughts, not reality, and that they are not a part of you. You can sometimes get so caught up validating your negative thoughts you don't want to let go of them. The bad feelings and negative thoughts become a part of a story that you tell other people. But they are still just a story and not reality. You were made for greatness, and any thought that does not inspire you to pursue your life's purpose is just a distraction.

You can use various strategies for getting rid of negative thoughts; you can see yourself having those crazy thoughts and laugh hysterically, or cancel those thoughts as soon as they show up, or write the negative thoughts on paper and toss the paper into the trash, or repeat a positive mantra that calms you. The bottom line is, you must decide to let go of the negative energy and the negative thoughts. You must decide to consistently generate positive and energized thoughts of being successful.

> You cannot entertain weak, harmful, negative
> thoughts ten hours a day and expect to bring about
> beautiful, strong, and harmonious conditions by
> ten minutes of strong, positive, creative thought.
> —Charles F. Haanel
> *The Master Key System*

Assignment Three

The assignment for step three is to visualize yourself achieving your goals. If you are very familiar with visualization, please tackle this exercise with a fresh new outlook. Make sure you are in a relaxed and quiet environment conducive to meditation. Initially, you may require a dark room and solitude, but eventually you will be able to do this visualization exercise anywhere you are. The ideal time for this exercise is before you go to bed at night and before you get up in the morning. But it will be effective whenever you have some quiet time to yourself.

Breathe deeply and slowly and relax each muscle in your body. You may put on meditation music if it relaxes you, but you should not use any music that has lyrics because they will be too distracting. Be aware of any tension in your body and focus on releasing the tension by relaxing your muscles and taking slow, deep breaths. Your experience will not be as effective if you do not completely relax. Take your time and be aware of the thoughts running through your mind. Don't try to control them; just be aware of them.

When you are ready, try to eliminate all thoughts. You may see white and dark space all around you. That means stop thinking about the kids, your work, and the bills that need to be paid; just put the whole world on hold for a few minutes. Initially, you may only be able to stop your thoughts completely for a few milliseconds. If you need help clearing your thoughts, visualize a broom in your mind and watch it as it sweeps all your thoughts away as quickly as they are coming to you. Once the broom has cleared all the clutter in your mind, put the broom away. This exercise makes you realize that on a conscious level, you have complete control of the thoughts that are processed in your mind.

Once your mind is clear, take time to create a futuristic image of yourself being wildly successful operating in your goals. The sky is the limit in this exercise. In this visualization, you want to see yourself making as much money as you want, having all the fame that you want, and achieving the level of success that you want. Make sure you have a clear picture of yourself in the future; ask yourself the following questions:

1. What clothes am I wearing?
2. What does my hair look like?
3. What jewelry am I wearing?
4. Am I standing or sitting?
5. What sounds do I hear around me?
6. What does the room or area around me look like?
7. Who is with me while I'm operating in my goal?
8. Do I see myself smiling and at peace?
9. What tasks am I completing and what expertise am I operating in?
10. What recognition am I receiving?
11. Who am I helping?
12. What problem do I see myself solving?

Once you have the visualization locked in your mind, make sure you replay this vision several times a day, week, and month. For example, if your goal was to write a number-one best seller, take time each day to see yourself at a book signing, see people coming up to you telling you how your book has had a positive impact on their life. See yourself thanking them for their kind words. Gratitude is the best emotion to experience when you are trying to draw in positive energy. Take time to get in touch with the way it feels making money as a best-selling author. Financial wealth is a realistic factor in achieving success. No one wants to be a poor number-one best-selling author. There is no limit to what you visualize as long as it creates positive energy and brings no harm to anyone else. As you see yourself operating in your goals, it should be clear why the goal is important to you and what your life is like now that the goal has been achieved.

If, on the other hand, you visualize negative things about your goals, like failing, you will only draw in negative energy. So, if at any time you have negative thoughts, cancel them immediately. If this happens often, it's time to connect with your goals partner and your higher power and find out what is blocking you from seeing yourself being successful. More than likely, fears are lingering in your subconscious, and once you identify them, you can use the techniques previously discussed to cancel them.

Remember, visualization should be used to allow your imagination to create a clear image, idea, or feeling that you wish to manifest. You must continue to use positive energy to focus on the ideas, feelings, or pictures of yourself achieving your goals until you achieve what you have been imagining. You were created to be successful at achieving your purpose. Therefore, anything that keeps you from success is a temporary roadblock that you first need to identify and then eliminate. You have the power within to create visions of successfully achieving the goals you set; at some point, with repeated visualizations and unwavering faith, those visions will start to manifest. When things start to manifest, you must be ready to take action.

You must form a clear and definite mental picture of what you want; you cannot transmit an idea unless you have it yourself.

> The more clear and definite you make your picture
> then, and the more you dwell upon it, bringing out all
> its delightful details, the stronger your desire will be.
> —Wallace D. Wattles
> *The Science of Getting Rich*

Step Four

The first part of step four is to remember step one through step three.

- Read books on relationships (at least fifteen minutes a day).
- Continue to build a thriving relationship with your goals partner.
- Spend time in prayer or meditation with your higher power.
- Read books that will help you improve your spiritual relationship to your higher power (at least fifteen minutes a day).
- Read and reread your short-term and long-term goals with excitement.
- Do visualization exercises on a daily basis. The exercise can last anywhere from one to forty minutes. Just don't stop there; at some point you must take action to create your goals.

The second part of step four is to find at least one person who has achieved at least one of your goals and study and model him or her. Studying does not mean stalking him or her! It means observing, viewing the person as your teacher or mentor. You can select someone you know personally or someone you have read or heard about, but it must be someone you admire so much that you are willing to research more than one resource to learn about his or her life. Make it a point to study this person's energy and skills that helped him or her create success. Also be sure to look at his or her achievements.

Do not look for his or her faults. Everyone has faults. What you are trying to do is focus on this person's positive characteristics so that you can draw those characteristics into your life.

> To fix your attention on the best is to surround
> yourself with the best, and to become the best.
> —Wallace D. Wattles
> *The Science of Getting Rich*

Getting Started: Step Four

The objective to step four is to appreciate and acknowledge the success of others so that you can attract that same success into your life. You can use the success of your model to visualize yourself operating at that same level of success. Just make sure you are not copying your mentor, but focusing on your own assignment and fulfilling you own purpose.

Say you want to be a number-one best-selling author, but you have to know what it takes to get in that position. So, the best thing to do is to find a best-selling author you admire and respect and research everything you can about him or her. Watch interviews; go online and find videos and news clips; use all your resources to find information. Where did he or she go to school? What other training did this author receive? How did he or she start writing? Did he or she have a big break? Look for any information about this author's success. See what you can learn from studying this best-selling author's path to success and what you can apply to your life and personal journey to success.

I once studied the path to success of one famous director who is also a writer, producer, and actor. He has done several interviews and I have seen the camera follow him behind the scenes of his movies. I felt he had innumerable characteristics that made him successful. Among his many talents, one characteristic stuck out in my mind—his ability to write. For me, writing appears to be his way of taking ideas, concepts, and messages that are in his heart and mind and sharing them with the world. That is what motivated me to write. I made a conscious decision to focus on writing and to see myself using writing as a way to share information and knowledge that has helped me excel and overcome challenges in my life.

> In every art beginners must start with models of those
> who have practiced the same art before them. And
> it is not only a matter of looking at the drawings,
> paintings, musical compositions, and poems that have
> been and are being created; it is a matter of being
> drawn into the individual work of art, of realizing
> that it has been made by a real human being, and
> trying to discover the secret of its creation.
> —Ruth Whitman

Assignment Four
The assignment for step four is to create a list of all the characteristics, skills, and talents that your model(s) possesses that led him or her to success in his or her field.

Review the list and visualize yourself possessing these skills with a high level of expertise. Talk to your goals partner and review your list of skills. Ask him or her to assist you in coming up with ways to professionally develop your skills so that you can operate in these talents with ease.

Research specific training, books, exercises, workshops, and classes that hone those skills. Your goals partner must become your accountability partner and make sure you are taking specific steps and strides toward improving your skills. Ask him or her to give you honest feedback and encouragement as you develop your skills.

If communication skills are on your list, be willing to do what it takes to develop those skills. You may think about joining a toastmasters group, comprised of professionals who come together to learn more about public speaking. These people challenge each other in a nurturing environment so that you are able to learn from your mistakes. If that seems too challenging, then find an organization or group you are passionate about and practice speaking up by making a suggestion or comment at least once during a meeting. If you are going to see yourself grow and obtain the skills that you need to be successful, you have to be willing to take risks.

If your talent is in a specialized field and you feel you are already an expert in that field, you can still learn from others, even if they do not have your level of success and expertise. Find the closest competitors in your field or people who are equally or more successful in a field that is similar to yours and observe their characteristics. It's amazing what you will learn about your industry and yourself when you observe your competition to see what they do well. Studying other people's paths to success is a great way to create your own road map to success.

> No man has yet become so great in any faculty but
> that it is possible for someone else to become greater.
> —Wallace Wattles
> *The Science of Being Great*

You may recall that in assignment two you were asked to write down short-term and long-term goals and to list steps to help you work toward achieving those goals. Well, now that you have begun developing your skills and talents, it's time to start putting those skills to use as you work through the steps you created in step two.

> By thought, the thing you want is brought
> to you. By action, you receive it.
> —Wallace D Wallace
> *The Science of Getting Rich*

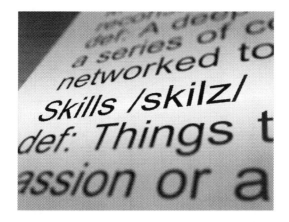

Step Five

The first part of step five is to remember step one through step four.

- Read books on relationships (at least fifteen minutes a day).
- Continue to build a thriving relationship with your goals partner.
- Spend time in prayer or meditation with your higher power.
- Read books that will help you improve your spiritual relationship to your higher power (at least fifteen minutes a day).
- Read and reread your short-term and long-term goals with excitement.
- Do visualization exercises on a daily basis. The exercise can last anywhere from one to forty minutes. Just don't stop there; at some point you must take action to create your goals.
- Find a model or mentor, someone you admire, who has successfully achieved one of your goals.
- Create a journal of his or her talents and skills and write about how those skills make him or her successful.

• Determine which classes, workshops, and lessons you need to take so that you can enhance your talents and skills and start utilizing your talents as you proceed through the steps you created in assignment two.

The second part of step five is to make the bold move and actually create something related to your goals or to take specific action toward achieving them. Review your list of goals and decide what you would like to create or do.

• Start a business or improve a current business.
• Start a ministry or expand a current ministry.
• Start a new profession or go back to an old profession.
• Volunteer for a company you may want to work for.
• Start a nonprofit organization or join a nonprofit organization.
• Start a team or join a team.
• Start an organization or join an organization.

• Write a book or a blog or sell articles you've written.
• Start an Internet business.
• Be on a TV show.
• Create a brochure or pamphlet of information and sell it on the Internet.
• Create a new invention.
• Make and sell jewelry.
• Sing in a musical play or CD.
• Become a photographer, painter, artist, or whatever strikes your fancy.

It can be anything you desire, but it has to be *something*. Nothing is more fulfilling than doing things you are passionate about. It's a bonus if you love what you do and it generates money at the same time. I'm not saying that you quit your job, but use your occupation and take the skills you have to start operating in your purpose. It's okay to start small, but make sure you connect your purpose to that business, profession, ministry, nonprofit organization, or team and make it something that you love. You may not have all the start-up capital you need to complete the items on your goals list, but I am certain that you can accomplish some part of your goal now. Even if it doesn't make you money right away, the work you start now could be saving you money in the future.

If you don't have all the qualifications you need to start your goal, decide to find a class, a workshop, an internship, or look up how-to videos on the Internet, or volunteer—whatever it takes to make sure you are doing things that enhance your skills relevant to your goals. Take the time to divide the ultimate goal into smaller steps and figure out which steps you can do now with minimal cost and the skills you already possess.

> Great things are not done by impulse, but by
> a series of small things brought together.
> —Vincent Van Gogh

Getting Started: Step Five
People go into industries or careers for various reasons: "I needed the money," "My family expected it," "It was easy for me," "This company was the only one that would hire me," "The work was close to my home." The list goes on

indefinitely. Most people take the path they feel is safe and prudent, but one day they wake up and life is just about over and they realize that they have missed their calling. How sad.

Doing things that are connected to your purpose and that you are passionate about allows you to live a fulfilled life. It is easier to get up every day and go to work. There's no better feeling than believing that one day you will achieve all the goals you desire and generate all the money you need.

Allow me to share a little of my story with you.

> When I first started with step five, I was a single mom with two kids. I had my own business doing accounting services for three large clients, which felt like having three jobs in one. I needed an assistant just to help me stay on top of the deadlines—and my life. I was busy, but I felt in my bones that I was missing something in life. I started looking at my goals list and decided to start doing small things from my list for at least fifteen minutes a day. Then life happened and I stopped completely. I had many family issues to address and started getting busier with my accounting services. The money really started coming in and my hours doing accounting work started to increase. My accounting services were making more money than ever, but this business was not my passion, and the sense that I was missing something in my life would not abate.

> One day, while I was out of state at a conference with one of my clients, one of the conference presenters made me reconnect to my passions instantly. It was such a

powerful moment that I felt compelled to put a twenty-dollar bill in the presenter's hand and thank him as I was leaving. I don't remember a word the presenter said, but I remember clearly how I felt when he spoke. The speaker had an anointing that motivated and inspired me. I truly believed that I could be successful if I just pursued my goals with an unwavering faith and determination. I spent the rest of the week in my hotel room in between sessions, using every spare moment to finish this guide. I took the time to create a task list for all my goals, and I started doing those tasks immediately. Below is a short sample of what I created:

1. Become a published writer.
   a. Finish writing my Goals Guide and find a publisher.
   b. Research background information for a guide on building relationships.
   c. Research the life and work of other writers of similar books.
   d. Read, read, and read works of other successful writers.
   e. Ask volunteers to read my guides in draft form for feedback.
   f. Visualize myself as a number-one best-selling author being interviewed by Oprah Winfrey.

2. Record a CD with my singing and sell thousands of CDs.
   a. Take singing lessons at a professional music studio.
   b. Set up my karaoke machine so that I can record myself singing.

    c. Learn new songs.

    d. Listen to other artists and study their techniques.

    e. Find a recording studio.

    f. Make recordings of my singing and post them on YouTube.

    g. Audition for a singing or talent competition.

3. Become a teacher or motivational speaker.

    a. Research where I can obtain a teaching credential or consider studying for a PhD so that I can teach at a college.

    b. Apply to part-time teaching jobs.

    c. Write a goals curriculum and offer "Goals Workshops."

    d. Volunteer at my son's charter school to observe other teachers.

Gradually, my excitement for life grew. I started practicing my singing everywhere—in the car, at the store, in the bathroom. I applied for several teaching positions although I had no idea when I would have time to teach. I even started to carry my laptop computer around so that I could work on this guide whenever I had a free moment. I started noticing that everywhere I went and everyone I spoke to gave me more information regarding my goals. I discovered messages, visions, and information that inspired me to complete this guide. My focus became my goals and my goals were connected to my purpose and not just my occupation. I started creating more time to do the things I was passionate about. Don't get me wrong, I enjoyed accounting and I always made sure that I had a steady income, but I used every spare moment as an opportunity to work on at least one task from my task list. The mere act of working on something that I loved, like this guide, made my life open up and become more fulfilling.

Making it a priority to spend at least thirty minutes a day working toward your goals is the most liberating feeling. It makes the mundane tasks of your life go by faster. Those of you who are thinking, "I have no time for this!" are completely incorrect. You have time for things you choose to have time for. You are in charge of your destiny.

> Don't say you don't have enough time. You have exactly the same number of hours per day that were given to Helen Keller, Pasteur, Michelangelo, Mother Teresa, Leonardo da Vinci, Thomas Jefferson, and Albert Einstein.
> —H. Jackson Brown Jr.,
> American author

Assignment Five

The assignment for step five is to create a list of tasks that will be needed to start your business, start an organization, write a book, pursue a new profession, or whatever that something is you want to do. Go over the details of your tasks list with your goals partner and create a realistic timeline that fits within your current schedule. You can go from zero to a hundred miles an hour *in your mind*. Put all those ideas on paper so that you can create a realistic and stress-free timeline you can follow.

Use your visualization exercises to see yourself operating in that something and make notes of all the details in your vision. Grab your journal and start writing. Initially, you will write whatever comes to mind; you will need to do some research to make sure you're not leaving out any important tasks or steps. The key here is to immediately get started doing something you love, something that leads you toward accomplishing your goals in a focused and organized manner.

> To accomplish great things we must first dream,
> then visualize, then plan . . . believe . . . act!
> —Alfred A. Montapert
> *The Supreme Philosophy of Man: The Laws of Life*

The task list you create needs to be very detailed. You should start by making sure you answer the standard who, what, when, where, why, and how questions. Here are some questions that need an answer while you are creating your task list:

- *Who* do you need to connect with to complete your task and achieve your goals? There are certain people and companies you may need to contact to work toward your goal.

_____

_____

_____

_____

- *What* action steps do you need to take? What things need to be done? What events should you attend or create? What is the purpose of your task and goals?

_____

_____

_____

_____

• *When* is the best time to do certain items? What is the order of things to complete? What timeline should you create?

_____

_____

_____

_____

• *Where* do your goals take place? Where do you need to go to research and achieve your goals?

_____

_____

_____

_____

• *Where* do you need to go to complete your task? Where can you find resources or learn more about your goals?

_____

_____

_____

_____

• *Why* are your goals important to you, your family, and the community? Why do you need to perform each task listed?

_____

_____

_____

_____

- *How* will each goal be achieved? How will progress be measured? How will you celebrate when you accomplish a significant task?

_____

_____

_____

_____

Step five is to make your goals a reality and to focus on the best and most organized way to reach your goals. You must have specific tasks listed so that you have a clear path to achieving your goals. It will be so rewarding when you are able to share the accomplishments of your goals with the universe. Absolutely everyone has something to offer and contribute, but it is important to know exactly what goals you are reaching for and how you are planning to get to them. If your goals are important to you, they are probably important to someone else. If you achieve your goals successfully, you have a duty to share your success with others.

When you have completed the questions in step five, ask your goals partner to help you stay focused. Create a timeline or put actual tasks on your calendar or planner. See if your goals partner can help you with any necessary research, with additional ideas for your task list, or even with handling some of the tasks. Keep your goals partner involved with your process so that he or she can motivate and encourage you along the way.

If you are doing these exercises alone, create a reward system for yourself. Make a list of things you enjoy doing or would like to purchase for yourself and reward yourself with something from that list each time you stay on track, complete a task, make significant progress toward a goal, or need additional encouragement.

Step Six

The first part of step six is to remember step one through step five.

- Read books on relationships (at least fifteen minutes a day).
- Continue to build a thriving relationship with your goals partner.
- Spend time in prayer or meditation with your higher power.
- Read books that will help you improve your spiritual relationship to your higher power (at least fifteen minutes a day).
- Read and reread your short-term and long-term goals with excitement.
- Do visualization exercises on a daily basis. The exercise can last anywhere from one to forty minutes. Just don't stop there; at some point you must take action to create your goals.
- Find a model or mentor, someone you admire, who has successfully achieved one of your goals.
- Create a journal of his or her talents and skills and write about how those skills make him or her successful.

- Determine which classes, workshops, and lessons you need to take so that you can enhance your talents and skills and start utilizing your talents as you proceed through the steps you created in assignment two.
- Make a detailed list of tasks and timelines needed to make your goals a reality.

The second part of step six is to get specific about the financial success you desire from achieving your goals and to create a budget. A budget is important so that you are able to put money toward your goals and to work toward creating financial security.

Despite what you may have heard, financial success makes achieving your goals worthwhile. Yes, it's wonderful to have goals that are a blessing to other people. But if you truly want to be a blessing to people, obtain financial resources that will allow you to do even more work for the enhancement of others.

If you are going to have a life filled with peace, satisfaction, and contentment, you need to feel financially secure. So to get specific about the financial success you desire, go back to your list of goals in step two and add the dollar amount you would expect to receive once you achieved each of these goals. When you look at your list and you see dollars beside each goal, you should feel a rush of excitement knowing that once you have achieved that goal, financial success will follow. If you feel any fear or doubt when you look at those numbers, it is likely that somewhere in your past you have connected negative feelings to money in general.

If that is the case, you will need to cancel those feelings. Having money in your hands should give you a positive feeling. Seeing a large balance in your bank account should make you feel confident and assured—not afraid that you may lose it. Talk to your goals partner and your higher power and be willing to look at the subconscious reasons that you connect fear or negativity with money. Once you identify those feelings, you can use various strategies for getting rid of those negative thoughts. Tell yourself that those thoughts are not real and money has been used for many good things in this world. Take a large bill of any amount, place it in your pocket, and hold it throughout the day. Each time you hold the money, smile and visualize what you could buy with that money. Make it a point to cancel any negative energy centered on money as it surfaces by shifting your thoughts to happy thoughts, shout out "I love money," or repeat a positive mantra that empowers you to strive to earn more money.

Getting Started: Step Six
Setting financial goals is just as important as setting any other goals. You have to create a picture of where you want your finances to be in the future. Once you are clear on where you want your finances to be, you can create a clear plan for getting there. Start by getting a good sense of your current financial situation by creating a budget and financial plan. You should have a sense of your current net worth. How much cash do you have on hand, and how much do you have in investments and equity?

Money should be something you value. Don't allow times to go by where you wonder where your money went. Become accountable for all the money that you receive. Give thanks for all the things you are able to do with the money you receive. Make paying bills a time of gratitude, because there is always someone less fortunate than you, someone who cannot do the things you are able to do. It does not matter how wealthy you are or how much money you think you don't have; as long as money is coming your way, you have a fiduciary responsibility to use it wisely.

Take time to write a formal budget or to write down your current monthly expenditures. Look at your bank statements or financial reports and review transactions. If you operate mostly in cash, save all your receipts for a month. The important thing is to review where your money is going and see if you can cut down on anything. Create a budget and make sure it includes a savings plan. Make sure you are accountable for every dollar or every million dollars that comes your way.

> Financial planning is the process of meeting your life
> goals through the proper management of your finances.
> —Certified Financial Planner Board of Standards

Assignment Six
The assignment for step five is to revamp your current goals list into a financial goals list and to create a budget for your current resources. Your financial goals list is simply taking your current goals list and including any financial rewards that you will receive once you achieve each of your goals. This may require you to think outside the box, because you may find it difficult to come up with an actual financial amount for each goal. You should take time to research how much money others have earned once they achieved these goals. Make an educated guess to start with realistic

expectations. It is important to note that some goals may not actually lead to generating money; however, this goal could save money or create an intrinsic value of a different kind. As an example, let's take a look at the previous goals list from step two.

Goal #1	Write an executive summary or a detailed description of what your construction business would look like, which people you would serve, and how the marketing would be done (check out examples of executive summaries on the Internet).	**$100 to $500 savings** The amount of money you will save if you write your own executive summary
Goal #2	Start a savings program to save funds toward the start-up cost (start an automatic transfer of a certain dollar amount into a separate investment account).	**$3,900 or more** The amount of money you could save in a year if you save $75 a week. You can do this by taking lunch to work, eating dinner at home, making your own coffee, and having movie night at home.
Goal #3	Research other ways to generate start-up capital for your construction business. • Use the Internet. • Go to my local bank. • Visit the Small Business Association (SBA).	**$1,000–$10,000** The amount of money you need as start-up capital for your business

Goal #4	Write a dynamic business or marketing plan for your construction business. The plan must provide a detailed description of your business, a description of the services offered, a market analysis, a marketing strategy, a summary of the management, and a financial plan for the first three to five years of operation along with a break-even analysis. This business plan will allow you to go to banks, investors, or even family and friends to request a start-up loan.	**$200,000** The amount of money you expect to generate in your first year of operation

Now that you have turned your goals list into a financial goals list, make it something wonderful to look at and post it somewhere you can see it every day. Decorate the financial goals list with things that interest you. Put real pictures of your goals on the list, add color, frame it, blow it up, or shrink it to a card size and carry it around in your pocket.

The second part of assignment five includes creating a real-life budget for your current finances using the table located at the end of step five. You are now shifting from visualizing your financial goals in the future to creating a budget for your current finances. If you already have a budget, take time to review it and see if it includes items needed to achieve your goals. If you don't have a budget, the list below will help you get started.

1. Rent or mortgage
2. Telephone
3. Cell phone
4. Utilities
   a. Gas
   b. Electric
   c. Water
   d. Sewer
5. Car insurance
6. Gasoline and transportation
7. Cable or satellite
8. Internet
9. Life insurance
10. Medical insurance
11. Savings
12. House and car repairs
13. Clothing and shoes
14. Laundry and cleaners
15. Medical bills
16. Spending money
17. Entertainment
18. Student loan
19. Car loan
20. Other loans
21. Credit cards
22. Tuition
23. Day care
24. Kids activities

This list is just a guide; there may be a lot more or different items you spend money on each month. As previously suggested, take a look at your bank statements and review each item. If you use cash, which can be an excellent way to budget, make sure you save receipts for everything you buy. This will allow you to monitor your budget. The focus here is to free up as much money as possible to put toward achieving your goals and creating financial security.

While you are creating your real-life budget, you might want to make sure that you set aside money for each of these categories:

- Ten percent tithes and charitable giving: When you are in a habit of giving, whether it's tithes, offerings, or charitable giving, make sure you do it with great excitement. The energy you create when you are giving to a person or organization that will benefit from your giving is very powerful; it opens the universe to return that same giving spirit back to you. In essence, you are creating the energy to receive more so that you can give more. If you make $10,000 a year and contribute 10 percent of your income, you can share $1,000 with others to make a difference in this world. However, if you make $1,000,000 a year and contribute 10 percent of your income, you can share $100,000. You can certainly affect more lives and make a greater impact if you are able to donate or tithe $100,000 rather than $1,000. So get connected to the idea that the more money you make the more money you can tithe or donate and the greater impact you will have for a larger number of people. It's a win-win situation for you and the universe.

- Ten percent savings and investing: Whether it's a dollar or a million dollars, putting money aside for yourself and your family is exciting. Make it a party and a celebration when you put money in your savings or investment account. I used to wake up every morning and transfer up to five dollars into my savings account. I would get excited to watch my savings grow, and it was an exciting way to start my day. Below are a few different types of savings that you can create.

o The most important type of savings is your unexpected-financial-event savings. This money should be set aside to address any unexpected expenses. These events aren't necessarily emergencies; they are simply not anticipated. Your car may break down unexpectedly and you may need extensive repairs or to put money down to purchase another vehicle. If you address the situation in a positive manner, you will view this as an opportunity to drive a newer and more reliable vehicle. This situation is only a devastating emergency if you were not prepared and do not have the funds to address the situation.

o A second type of savings is for retirement. This money is intended to secure your future when you are at an age when you no longer can or don't want to work as much. An adequate retirement will ensure that all of your needs will be met even when your monthly income decreases or when you stop working altogether.

o A third type of savings is for entertainment and fun purchases. Setting aside cash to buy that one thing you have always wanted rather than financing that purchase will save you a lot of money and stress. If you finance something you cannot really afford, you have to pay it off over time, and the interest you will pay could have been used to purchase something else you may have always wanted or needed. So, if you want to take a vacation or buy a boat, create a savings plan so that you do it debt-free.

 • Ten percent play money: Play money is money from your paycheck you use for entertainment and miscellaneous expenses. It is no fun when all of your income is needed to pay bills. Life should include fun activities you enjoy. However, it's also important that your play money is not your whole paycheck. Now is the time to balance things. It is very stressful to party your check away and then worry about paying your rent or mortgage and utilities, and deal with bill collectors calling 24-7. A good balance is to use about 10 to 20 percent of your income for relaxation and fun, while using the rest wisely.

- Seventy percent bills: Paying bills is only stressful when your monthly expenses exceed the revenue you have coming in. When you complete assignment five and create a budget for your current finances, you will know just where you stand. It can be an eye-opening experience when you take time to write down every monthly expense and compare it to your monthly revenue. It is also important not to take on additional financial obligations if you do not have a consistent cash flow. Finally, be careful to not take on any debt or long-term obligations that cannot be easily eliminated. Living within your means makes it so easy to spend your time focusing on making and receiving more money.

Once you have completed your budget, discuss your current financial situation with your goals partner and determine ways to make it better. You can discuss answers to the following questions:

1. Do I live within my monthly budget? If not, why?

   _____

   _____

2. If I were able to eliminate a few monthly expenditures, how much money could I put into savings toward my goals?

   _____

   _____

3. What do I need to set up an automatic savings plan? If I already have an automatic savings plan, what do I need to do to increase the amount so that I can set aside additional funds toward achieving my goals?

    _____

    _____

4. How can things on my goals list help me increase my income each month? How can I increase my income so that I can do things that are on my goals list?

    _____

    _____

The work with your goals partner will require that you start implementing changes in the way you think and operate financially. If you require additional funds to achieve your goals, a savings plan is essential. It doesn't matter how much or how little money you make; make sure you have control of your finances so that you can live a goals-fulfilled life with a sense of financial security for the future.

> Many people take no care of their money
> till they come nearly to the end of it, and
> others do just the same with their time.
> —Johann Wolfgang von Goethe

MONTH

	First Pay
Income	
Paycheck #1	
Paycheck #2	
Other Business Income	
Total Monthly Income	-
Monthly Bills	
Installment / Revolving Agreements	
Total Monthly Exp	-
Net CashFlow	-

Step Seven

The first part of step seven is to remember step one through step six.

- Read books on relationships (at least fifteen minutes a day).
- Continue to build a thriving relationship with your goals partner.
- Spend time in prayer or meditation with your higher power.
- Read books that will help you improve your spiritual relationship to your higher power (at least fifteen minutes a day).
- Read and reread your short-term and long-term goals with excitement.
- Do visualization exercises on a daily basis. The exercise can last anywhere from one to forty minutes. Just don't stop there; at some point you must take action to create your goals.
- Find a model or mentor, someone you admire, who has successfully achieved one of your goals.
- Create a journal of his or her talents and skills and write about how those skills make him or her successful.

- Determine which classes, workshops, and lessons you need to take so that you can enhance your talents and skills and start utilizing your talents as you proceed through the steps you created in assignment two.
- Make a detailed list of tasks and timelines needed to make your goals a reality.
- Discuss your financial goals with your goals partner and create a balanced budget where you tithe, save, have fun, and pay bills timely.

The second part of step seven is to make sure you have identified goals you are absolutely passionate about. It may seem like this step should be number one, but it's not—for a good reason. Step seven is designed to provide you with a deeper level of clarity about yourself, your true passions, and your life. You would be surprised to see how many people tackle things on autopilot or because it's what they've always done or because they want to fulfill the dreams of others. That is not why or for whom this guide was created. This guide is for people who want to step beyond the norm to pursue goals they are truly passionate about.

You have just taken time out of your life to read this guide, do the exercises, and get started on accomplishing some of your goals. Now is the time to make sure you are on the right track. It's time to assess what you read and retained. Let's find out if the goals you chose are really what you are most passionate about. This guide will not be effective if you are successful in achieving goals just for the sake of achieving goals. This guide is designed to get you to a place where you live in excitement every day, where you wake up in the morning and say "I love my life."

Background to Step Seven

We live in a time of amazing opportunities brought to us by way of computers and technology. There are millions of ways to make money doing things that you love. For example, the opportunities for an artist today are unlimited. Artists no longer have to limit their artwork to paper or canvas for watercolors, oil painting, or black-and-white sketches. Artists today can get involved in computer-aided graphic arts and design, which opens so many vistas for artistic expression *and* marketing.

What if you always wanted to open a retail business? You no longer have to have a storefront business and worry about rent and utility costs every month. You can start selling your products from a custom website with very little start-up cost. The business opportunities in this computer age are limitless. So, when you think about the things you love to do, make sure you take the blinders off and look beyond the traditional way of doing things.

Assignment Seven

This is the final exercise! The assignment for step seven is to create a different list. This is a fun list of at least ten things that you *really* want to do in life. It is similar to a bucket list, but let's call it a what-I-really-want-to-do-while-I'm-still-livin' list. Before you start this list, take a moment to think about those things that you have always wanted to do and make sure they are not too fantastical, but actual things you want and can do.

For example: If you always wanted to sing in a televised singing competition but know you would never have the courage to get in front of millions of people and belt out a tune, you could record a video of yourself singing and post it on the Internet. You could also make a studio recording of a song you wrote and make a music video. You could also sing at a senior assisted living facility, your church, or get out there and get a gig at a night club. The important thing is that you separate your realistic aspirations and dreams from unrealistic fantasies.

Your what-I-really-want-to-do-while-I'm-still-livin' list should also be very specific. Don't just say, "I want to travel to the Fiji Islands." What do you know about Fiji? Go online and research what you can find out about the islands. What is it that you expect to see or do while you are there? Will this really make you happy and fulfilled? Sometimes we get into a rut of desiring things because others desire them, but we never really bothered to make sure that they really suit our desires and needs.

Once you have written your list of at least ten items, review them with your goals partner. This part of the exercise really should not be done alone, so if you don't yet have a goals partner, ask a friend or someone you trust to do this exercise with you. Together, you are going to read each item one at a time and discuss the details involved. Tell him or her why you want to do these things and what it would mean to do these things while you are still living. After you have gone over each item on your list, pick the top three.

Your goals partner will then read the first two of the top three items and ask you which one is more important to you. More important in this context means that life will not be the same if you do not achieve the item. Visualize yourself doing both items and listen to your heart. Ask yourself which one brings you the most joy. Once you decide if item one or item two is more important, compare that item with item three and do the same exercise again. Visualize yourself doing the third item and determine which item is more important now. In the end, you will have identified the number-one thing that you really want to do while you are still living. It is the one thing that supersedes everything else.

Now take your number-one item and review your goals list you created in step two. Does your number-one item correlate to anything on your goals list? It could be an exact match or it could be something related to one of your goals. If the one thing you want to do while you're still living is nowhere on your goals list, you must ask yourself some hard questions about how to reconnect to your true passions and desires in life. The goals do not have to match exactly; however, your goals and the passions that you want to experience while you are still living should be related.

If they are not, go back to step two and redo your goals list by including things from your what-I-really-want-to-do-while-I'm-still-livin' list. This time you will complete step two through step five with more passion and zeal, because you are 100 percent clear about your goals and you know they must be achieved. Reconnect with your goals partner and discuss what you have found about yourself and discuss how your new set of goals is directly connected to your what-I-really-want-to-do-while-I'm-still-livin' list.

If item one from your what-I-really-want-to-do-while-I'm-still-livin' list matches one of your goals from step two, you have discovered a goal that you must achieve while you are living. Start with that goal first! Even if you don't ever fully achieve this goal, it's better to spend the rest of your life having fun working these steps and trying to get there.

Once you have completed the number-one thing you really want to do in life, proceed to numbers two and three, making sure they are listed somewhere on your goals list. Go through steps two through five as many times as you need or want to. Your life will never be the same if you don't even make an effort to achieve at least the first three things on your what-I-really-want-to-do-while-I'm-still-livin' list.

> A year ago, one of my readers, Lee, read the entire guide in draft form and was starting to experience success with some of the goals he had listed. But once he completed step seven, he realized he was missing something. Although he was living a passion-filled life, was enjoying his career success, and was having success with his current goals, he discovered he was even more passionate about being a stand-up comedian than his current career. So he went back to step two of this guide and focused on his new goal. Working through steps two through seven was much easier the second time around. He started working on a comedy routine, learned the successful tactics, researched the lives of other comedians, purchased a book on stand-up comedy, made a list of steps needed to look for opportunities to do his routine, and found a goals partner who actually knew someone in the business.
>
> One day, while continuing to work the steps of this guide, Lee heard about a neighborhood watch

meeting. He contacted the head of the neighborhood watch and asked if he could do his comedy routine during the meeting. A few weeks later I received an invitation from Lee to the neighborhood watch meeting. The flyer announced: Entertainment provided by guest comedian: Lee Johnson. I could only imagine how excited Lee felt because he himself actively created this opportunity. I attended the neighborhood watch meeting, and I laughed so hard during his routine I cried. Everyone who watched fell in love with Lee. I never even knew he possessed those skills, but I could tell he had put a lot of time and research into his routine. I could also tell he was truly living his passion.

The time is now. Take action. You have everything within you to achieve the most phenomenal success ever. Now you also have a guide that provides you with a clear and concise recipe to create your own road map to your goals.

> You may not feel certain that you will succeed
> today, or next week, but you must feel certain
> that you will succeed sometime.
> —Wallace D. Wattles
> *The Science of Getting Rich*

The world has enough room for your success, my success, and the success of everyone else who chooses to operate in a life filled with purpose and goals. By now, you should have heard your higher power speaking to you. After all, this is where all your wonderful ideas ultimately come from.

> We grow great by dreams. All big men are dreamers.
> They see things in the soft haze of a spring day
> or in the red fire of a long winter's evening.
> Some of us let these great dreams die, but others
> nourish and protect them; nurse them through
> bad days till they bring them to the sunshine and
> light which comes *always* to those who sincerely
> hope that their dreams will come true.
> —Woodrow Wilson

In the beginning of this guide, I challenged you to read this book, do the assignments, and note where your life was before you followed the steps and where your life should be thirty to ninety days after you finish reading the guide. Once you have reached any level of success, e-mail me your story at jandjacquisitions@gmail.com and tell me about the steps you took and the goals you achieved. I am going to post the most inspiring stories on my website. You never know, your success story just might be a blessing to someone else.

SUCCESS
EFFORT
MANAGEMENT
PLANNING
KNOWLEDGE
RESEARCH
GOALS

About the Author

Onyx Jones, once a homeless single mother, is now a successful entrepreneur who has a master's degree in accounting. Onyx has written many effective procedure manuals for her clients, but this guide is a reflection of the steps she took to create a life filled with passion. Today, Onyx has an amazing husband and three children.

Printed in the United States
By Bookmasters